Minimalism

A Primer On Minimalism For Novices A Simple And Systematic Manual For Achieving A Streamlined, Reoriented, And Uncomplicated Lifestyle

(Methods Employed By Contemporary Individuals To Reduce Stress Include Decluttering, Organizing Their Living Spaces, And Practicing Digital Minimalism)

Vanda António

TABLE OF CONTNET

How To Take A Minimalist Vacation 1

Decide Which Electronics You'll Bring. 8

Clear Out Your Computer And Mobile Devices 24

Creating And Sustaining Connections While Traveling 40

Storage Areas: Garage, Basement, And Attic 63

Why So Many Individuals Are Only Able To Split Ways With Sorrow? 80

Changing One's Attitude And Discovering Balance 101

Prioritise Needs Over Wants By Focusing On Essential Expenses. 116

Have You Set A Time Restriction For The Meeting? 146

How To Take A Minimalist Vacation

Being minimalist goes beyond simply clearing out clutter from your house and workstation. It's also about seeing the world and traveling without bringing too much.

True happiness might be impeded by the need to possess material possessions. It can slow down your exploration and keep you from moving freely. However, you can save money by purchasing less expensive flights when you travel minimally. You can travel in more safety and convenience. You can have a far greater cultural experience, lower your chance of theft, and prevent waiting for too much baggage to arrive.

Many people find it challenging to pack light. You will understand that you don't need a lot of stuff to survive, though, once you've trained yourself to pack lighter and wiser. Packing like a doomsday survivalist is not necessary. All you need is one carry-on bag to get you through.

Traveling minimalistically starts with having the appropriate mindset.

You must decide to live a minimalist lifestyle with this objective in mind. You must train yourself to think and act properly. This is the first issue that needs to be resolved. You will never be able to commit to this lifestyle unless you are ready to give up your old habits of piling up junk.

To travel and live in this manner, you must acclimate yourself. Don't try to force it. You must learn to feel at ease with simplicity. It should be possible for you to distinguish between needs and wants. You can become a Minimalist traveler in this way.

Fill a tiny bag with sensible items.

Don't acquire a big bag so you won't be tempted to bring extra stuff.

When they notice their luggage has extra room, many people want to carry more stuff. Therefore, you should purposefully select a tiny bag to avoid this. You'll have to pack lightly if there isn't much room available. However, be sure to leave a fourth of your bag unfilled. In this manner, you'll have enough room to load and unload rapidly and to accommodate any purchases you make while traveling. The typical capacity of a carry-on bag is between forty and forty-five liters. This should be sufficient if you intend to stay in a hotel and not pitch a tent. The majority of hotels provide everything you would need for your journey. Therefore, you don't need to pack that much stuff.

A backpack is a better option than rolling luggage if you are taking a longer trip than a quick flight. Using wheeled luggage on cobblestone streets, sandy beaches, old staircases, and dirt roads is challenging. Backpacks are also functional. They are readily stowed under bus seats, tossed in the back of trucks, or locked inside lockers. They also include features that can greatly simplify packing and organizing.

Find out how to travel with less stuff on your next trip. Asking yourself which goods from your last vacation were rarely used or unused is a solid rule of thumb. You've shown yourself that you can travel without these things, so don't bring them. Similarly, you must decide which behaviors have proven unnecessary and can be eliminated from your daily routine. Additionally, you want to ascertain whether there are any scaled-down equivalents of the items you usually pack for travel. Consider packing travel-sized toothpaste, shampoo, deodorants, and other necessities instead of full-sized ones.

You ought to be aware of which goods are necessary as well. Typically, these items include your ID, passport, money, credit cards, charger, spare batteries, and smartphone. Not having these things with you can make travel challenging. Therefore, make sure you pack them first to prevent forgetting them.

After you've placed them in your bag, you should add further necessities. A sweater or jacket, cozy shoes, makeup, and clothing are some examples. Multipurpose items, like a bottle that serves as both a shampoo and a conditioner, are always helpful to have with you. Remember to pack a water bottle so you can stay hydrated.

Don't be afraid to underpack as well; very rarely will you find yourself in a scenario where you can't find an unexpected item you truly need. However, if you find yourself stranded in a strange place where you don't speak the language and need a dress shirt that night, let that be part of the journey. I promise you, it's an experience rather than a problem.

Decide Which Electronics You'll Bring.

You must travel with a smartphone unless you intend to live off the grid. To use a map or GPS, take photos and movies to record your travels, communicate with others, access the Internet, and capture images and films, you need a smartphone.

You might use your phone or tablet instead of the expensive equipment if you're not a professional photographer or videographer. DSLRs are more of a luxury than a necessity.

You only need a phone, headphones, and a battery or charger. You might also need to bring a laptop if you have work to do. Alternatively, you could use a tiny netbook or pair your smartphone with a Bluetooth keyboard.

How to Stow Your Bag

Packaging for your trip at least one day in advance is a good idea. You can prevent rushing and neglecting anything in this way. Utilize all of the compartments that are provided as well.

The Principal Divide

Clothes and smaller bags, pouches, or packing cubes should be stored here. Additionally, rolled-up clothing is far easier to see and reach for than folded clothing.

Packing cubes are useful for smaller goods like socks and undergarments. They let you keep these necessities apart to quickly get them when needed. You can also use pouches to keep your toiletries from getting lost among your clothes and bulkier stuff. Additionally, storing them in a pouch lessens the possibility of shampoos, conditioners, etc. leaking.

You can tie an extra pair of shoes to your backpack or store them in a shoe bag. You can fit extra food or souvenirs in your luggage on your way back if you tie your rubber or sneakers to it.

You might also wish to think about shoe substitutes. For instance, you might just pack a pair of flip-flops or canvas sneakers that you can fold up. There is not much space required for this kind of shoes. They might, however, only be appropriate in specific areas and during specific seasons.

You might need to pack extra clothes if you are going somewhere cold. Wearing the coat or jacket instead of packing it in your backpack is a solid rule of thumb. In case it rains, you should also pack a lightweight raincoat. Use a compression bag if you must pack various clothes to conveniently store the things you no longer require.

You can leave your pajamas at home if you are heading somewhere sunny and warm. You can simply wear your shorts and tank top to bed. It's entirely up to you whether or not to use this extra room for your swimsuit.

The Front Divide

To avoid packing your toiletries within the main section, you might use the front compartment of your bag to hold them. It can also hold other tiny towels, handkerchiefs, or other useful items. Since microfiber dries faster and is lighter than standard cotton, it's better to use one for travel.

Remember that the amount of liquids you can bring in your carry-on is limited to 100 ml. Therefore, you might use solid soap and shampoo bars rather than liquid soap and shampoo. They weigh less and are more portable.

Furthermore, 90% of liquid soaps are more effective because they are made of water.

Shampoo bars function similarly to soap bars. Shampoo turns frothy when a shampoo bar is rubbed in water. Your shampoo bar can last up to a year if you don't wash your hair daily. It can last many months. However, you can put your preferred liquid soap and shampoo into travel-sized bottles if you want to bring them. These receptacles are available at your neighborhood pharmacy.

In addition to toiletries, you may store a small inflatable pillow in the front section of your suitcase. It doesn't require a lot of room. It's not rubbery, even if you have to blow it up. It is cozy and comfortable for naps.

If you intend to visit a beach, you might also wish to pack a waterproof bag.

Chapter 8: The Whole Understanding of a Minimalist Way of Life

As we approach the conclusion of this little tutorial, I'd like to take a moment to explain what a fully minimalist lifestyle comprises. It's all about freedom, as the chapter title makes clear.

The exact opposite of a shackle that would prevent you from reaching your goals is what minimalism is intended to do. Furthermore, minimalism is not this sometimes misconstrued ideology that advocates for "the less you have, the better." That's not all the depth it possesses. The fundamental goal of minimalism as a worldview is freedom—the feeling of emancipation we experience when we eliminate excesses from our lives. Minimalism can be viewed as a framework that exposes and clarifies the elements necessary to achieve the freedom we discuss. Because of this, it gives every one of us the chance to develop into persons free from excess and willing to share our inner selves.

I now realize that everyone has their unique style of doing things, as well as likes, dislikes, pet peeves, and, most importantly, aspirations and anxieties. However, we cannot ignore the reality that, at our heart, the working conditions for all of us are the same. Although we may have unique tastes, we are all the same because we have preferences. And that's precisely where the perspective of minimalism finds its usefulness. This can all benefit us in some manner because it is a movement based on core ideas.

When things are clear, we can judge them for what they are, which helps us make our own decisions. We are endowed with the courage to muster our strength and maintain our composure in the face of excess. We also firmly establish ourselves in our reality as people by remaining composed.

As I stated at the outset, this is not a manual that will tell you what to do every single step of the way and then miraculously improve your life. This guideline is a work of literature meant to assist rather than dictate.

Being in the world is incredibly fascinating. Without wanting to sound cliche, things might not always go your way—in fact, they might even be nasty at times—but they never stop trying to get your attention. That being said, we have the ability and capacity to choose how we react to the situations that life throws at us. The fact that even our apathy is a reaction in and of itself brings us to my main conclusion: we are here, and it is entirely up to us to determine how the world turns out.

It will be a journey for you now, and I wish you the best. If you maintain and demonstrate the core principles of minimalism, you should eventually achieve success, even if you haven't decided what your objective is yet. Or maybe you've sorted everything out and are ready for this adventure. All the same, I want the best for you.

Chapter 8: A Clutter-Free Life

For many, living a simpler, clutter-free existence can be appealing. There are undoubtedly many advantages to having fewer belongings, such as lower debt and less to maintain, worry about, and arrange. Living a minimalistic lifestyle allows you to spend all the extra money you've saved on the things you want to do. Many find living a simpler, clutter-free life with fewer possessions appealing.

But one point has to be addressed: where should you start? Thinking about working step by step and using a checklist to help you through this process before you become overwhelmed and stressed is a good idea.

Clear Out Your Spaces

Your living quarters, specifically your bedroom, are a good place to start if you're on a decluttering campaign. You should start caring for yourself here as this is where you spend most of your time. A list of items to keep in mind when decluttering your rooms is provided below:

To remove any clutter from a counter, clean it.

Select a shelf and purge everything that isn't needed.

Choose five items from your stash that you use frequently and arrange them properly.

Spend some time envisioning the space and determining your goals.

Load up your car with extras and donate them to a good cause.

Put everything that breaks straight in the trash bag.

Make a 30-day plan to tidy up one item at a time.

Arrange bowls and trays on your dressing tables to catch clutter and hold any little items you could lose.

Sort Through Your Clothes

Admit it: most of us have awful closets filled with unnecessary items, out-of-style items, and shoes. Most of the time, the thought of parting with an expensive item you never intended to wear keeps you from clearing out your closet of items you'll never wear. You can begin the process of retaining just items that you truly want on you by using this checklist:

Empty the wardrobe of all items of clothing, shoes, and accessories.

Sort and store all of your non-used clothing and footwear.

After gathering every article of clothing in your home, determine whether to keep it or give it away.

To prevent keeping items that you no longer like in your closet, it's a good idea to try your clothes on before putting them back.

Clear Out Your Workspace

You spend most of your time in your office, just like your home. Some of us may even consider it our second home, spending more time there than anywhere else. In such cases, it may become our home rather than vice versa. We tend to fill our time at work with unneeded activities as we spend more time there, which lowers our productivity and makes us look messy.

Because we have established a comfort zone at work, we also tend to have more crowded workstations after extended periods of employment. The following to-do list will assist you in tidying up your workspace and positively influencing your coworkers:

Get rid of everything deemed "trash," such as empty pens, old notes, paper cups, and used paper.

Get rid of all those mountains of paper by going through them and retaining only the important documents. Store private documents with caution in drawers and separate files.

Ensure the cables are neat and organized, and check if any dust has lodged in your computer's keyboard.

On the wall of your workstation, avoid overhanging pictures, post-its, and other notes.

Upon completion of each shift, tidy your workstation.

Clear Out Your Computer And Mobile Devices

Recall that we began by discussing how our gadgets play a major role in the materialism and cluttered lifestyle surrounding us. To be clear, we did not want to imply that you should throw away your gadgets immediately (after all, this ebook was written on one and was intended to be seen on one at the end of the day). Rather, we want you to eliminate the clutter and preserve the items that are important to you and contribute value to your life. This to-do list will be very beneficial to you as you clear up your devices and everything inside of them:

Remove all of the subscriptions you don't need in your life.

Make clearing out your inbox a time-consuming, one-week task. Save only emails that are truly important to you, and go through each folder one at a time. Get rid of all the pointless files and downloads from your desktops, and save only the folders and files that are important to you. Arrange all helpful items into organized folders to save time and prevent inconveniences.

Remove any software and apps you no longer require on your devices.

To enhance the functionality of your devices and browsers, keep the caches emptied. You should also maintain them uncluttered.

Disable all pointless alerts on your phone.

Disable any unused screensavers and visual effects.

Make a backup of all the large files and place them in folders on memory cards and external hard drives.

Declutter Your Kitchen: People often want to keep pointless items in their kitchens. Have you ever seen those crammed refrigerators full of the most pointless things you can imagine, some of which are past or near expiration? That may apply to you, though, as consumerism has led to a tendency among humans to store things well ahead of need. Buying just items that you want to consume soon is the minimalist way of living. Eating fresh food can improve your health because you will only be eating fresh food. It can also significantly lower your electricity costs because it will put less strain on your refrigerator and make it easier to chill food. The following to-do list will assist you in clearing out your kitchen and eating habits:

Imagine what you would like your kitchen to look like; you might even sketch up a basic layout on paper.

Keep food away from items like soaps and detergents, and keep worktops spotless.

Empty your refrigerator and freezer, preserving only anything that hasn't gone bad. Get rid of all those jam jars and open mostly used bean cans.

Empty your cupboard and put all your spices and herbs in labeled, transparent jars.

Ensure the preparation area is spotless, including the worktops surrounding the stove and oven.

Put your cleaning supplies together and keep them on a different shelf to one side.

Discard any used cutlery, utensils, and plates; alternatively, donate them to a worthy cause.

Clear Out Your Social Network

For some of us, this may be a challenging one. Humans tend to be stubborn and don't like to give up on others, which might harm our development. Now, we're not saying that you should cease communicating with the friends and family that are important to you. Instead, we advise giving up on other "fluff" people to spend more time with those truly important in your life. We have begun to take the opinions of individuals who shouldn't matter to us far more seriously than we should, which is one major factor contributing to the rise of consumerism. Viewing their friends' Facebook pages and Snapchat stories, they are more likely to experience depression due to the jealousy that these platforms arouse. Put an end to your worries! If you just strictly adhere to this checklist, you will soon have a decluttered social life:

Recognize your priorities and use them to categorize the people in your immediate vicinity.

Maintain a structured routine and avoid overcommitting to other activities to spend more time with your pals.

Keep a calendar and a list to determine whether you are spending enough time with the people and things that are important to you and/or where you need to make improvements.

Use social media only when necessary. Facebook and Instagram's pointless scrolling will take time and, worse, make you feel insecure or envious of others.

Sort your buddy groups based on significance and allot attention to each one appropriately.

Get rid of those who only stalk you on social media and whom you perceive as "baggage."

Above all, make an effort to appreciate a clutter-free living. You may find far more time to concentrate on the things, people, and experiences that truly mean to you if you do this correctly, even though it can take some time and work. We truly feel that it might be highly contagious with all the extra time, money, and space you have to try new things in life if you get the hang of it. While not comprehensive, the checklist above should provide a solid grasp of the mindset you should adopt for all aspects of your life and every decision you make.

Chapter 7: Easier Living through Simplifying Meals and Eating Habits

Convenience food and sugary drinks are what we typically choose, and this can result in diabetes, heart disease, and weight gain. Nonetheless, by simplifying the things you eat and how you prepare them, a minimalist lifestyle might assist you in forming healthy eating habits.

Minimalism for your general health and well-being by streamlining your meals and eating routines. We will also offer helpful hints for organizing your pantry, streamlining meal preparation, and preparing wholesome meals.

Make Your Pantry Simpler

To start making your meals simpler, clear out your cupboard. Sort through your pantry and discard any bad or expired items. Chips, candies, and processed snacks fall under this category. Rather, stock your cupboard with healthful and nutrient-dense items like beans, nuts, seeds, and whole grains.

Purchasing in bulk is another way to streamline your pantry. You'll save costs, reduce waste, and guarantee that you always have the components you need when you shop in bulk. Brown rice, oats, dry beans, and quinoa are a few excellent bulk things to consider.

Cut Down on Food Wastage

Minimizing food waste is just another crucial component of minimalist dining. Make a meal plan in advance and just purchase what you will need.

Additionally, you can repurpose your leftovers to create inventive dishes. For instance, leftover chicken might be used in soups, salads, or sandwiches the next day. You may add leftover veggies to frittatas or stir-fries. In the kitchen, use your imagination, and don't be scared to attempt new things!

Easy Planning and Preparation of Meals

Preparing and organizing meals is a crucial aspect of minimalist eating. Every week, set aside some time to plan your meals and go grocery shopping for the necessary supplies. This will cut down on the time you spend in the kitchen and simplify your meals.

Using a meal planning app or website is one method to make meal planning easier. With these apps, you can make grocery lists, plan your meals, and even get recipe ideas based on the components you already have. Plan to Eat, Mealime, and CookSmart are a few of the well-liked meal-planning applications.

Cooking in batches will make meal preparation and meal planning easier. This entails preparing large quantities of food that can be consumed all week long. As an illustration, you might prepare a big pot of chili or soup that you could eat for lunch or dinner all week long. Large quantities of baked items, such as bread or muffins, can be prepared and frozen for later use.

Prepare Healthful Meals

Lastly, prepare wholesome meals to streamline your diet and create healthier eating habits. This entails choosing unprocessed, whole foods, including fruits, vegetables, whole grains, and lean meats.

To create wholesome meals, use basic culinary methods like grilling, roasting, and sautéing. These methods bring out the inherent tastes in your food while also making cooking easier.

To ensure you get all the nutrients you require, include a variety of foods in your diet. Try different cuisines and flavors, such as exotic fruits or vegetables, to keep your meals interesting and engaging.

In summary

In conclusion, you can significantly improve your general health and well-being by simplifying mealtimes and eating habits. A healthier and more sustainable lifestyle can be achieved by clearing out your pantry, cutting down on food waste, streamlining meal planning, and preparing wholesome meals. Recall that cutting back on ingredients in your meals doesn't have to imply compromising taste or diversity. Explore your culinary creativity while reaping the rewards of a more purposeful and healthy way of living.

Creating And Sustaining Connections While Traveling

Being a digital nomad and networking.

For many of us digital nomads, networking is our lifeblood. It's not just about passing business cards back and forth; it's also about exchanging information and advice, which come in handy while you're on the go. A wealth of knowledge may be found from other nomads, who can suggest everything from safe havens for travelers to dependable co-working spaces and Wi-Fi locations.

It also involves working together on tasks. While traveling, you may encounter other experts who could inspire new company initiatives or even intriguing partnership prospects. You never know when a friendly discussion could develop into a business collaboration. And there's the societal dimension. Let's face it: living a nomadic lifestyle can sometimes be isolating. Developing friendships and keeping a busy social life requires networking. It guarantees you have a community wherever you are and prevents the journey from getting overly solitary.

Another benefit of networking is staying current. Being a part of a network keeps you up to date with the always-changing landscape of remote work, from new tools to altered visa restrictions. It's similar to keeping an eye on the most recent advancements. Remember the local knowledge. Conversation with locals and other nomads can help you discover the subtleties of the area, undiscovered attractions, and proper business conduct. It's an insider's perspective that many guidebooks don't provide.

And lastly, the component of mental and emotional support. Although living a nomadic lifestyle is exciting, it has difficulties. In difficult circumstances, a network offers a group of people who know exactly what you're going through, acting as a support system. Networking is a complex asset that enhances our personal and professional lives, making it more than just a professional tool for digital nomads. Although opinions on its significance could differ, most people agree that it's an important part of the community of digital nomads.

Maintaining contact: Simplified tools for optimal immersion.

A key component of the nomadic lifestyle, personally and professionally, is maintaining ties. Less is frequently more in our society, especially regarding the devices we use to stay in touch. Here are several simple ways to stay in touch that will ensure you stay connected to the outside world without having to deal with excessive platforms or gadgets.

Without a question, your smartphone serves as your communication Swiss Army knife. After making sure it's prepared for usage abroad, simplify your applications. Most of your needs can be met by multipurpose ones like WhatsApp, which allows for phone, video, and text chatting. Telegram and Viber are also excellent.

Less is more in social media terms. Remain on one or two social media sites, such as Facebook or Instagram, to stay in touch with your loved ones.

A sturdy, lightweight laptop or tablet is essential if your profession requires a larger screen. Combine your personal and business email accounts into a single primary account. Tools for video conferences, such as Zoom or Google Meet, are useful for both business and family catch-ups.

Invaluable for saving memories and crucial documents without requiring physical space.

Virtual post mail services are a blessing for people who require a fixed address because they can handle everything from check depositing to mail scanning.

Even though Wi-Fi is widely available, you may always stay connected with a local SIM card or an international roaming service like Google Fi. A portable Wi-Fi gadget can come in quite handy in more isolated areas.

The newest tool for networking is digital business cards. You may easily communicate your contact information without carrying a stack of cards by using apps like Hello.

Your actual notebooks can be replaced with note-taking applications like Evernote or Notion, which are ideal for taking notes, creating lists, and keeping a journal.

You need a reliable calendar app to manage your schedule across time zones. You can use an Apple or Google calendar to help you remember appointments and private occasions.

Additionally, bookworms can save valuable luggage rooms by carrying a library in their pockets with an e-reader or tablet software.

To sum up, digitization and consolidation are key. Use multifunctional tools and embrace digital substitutes for tangible goods.

Finding the ideal setting could take some time, but these simple strategies can support you in keeping deep connections without becoming overburdened.

What is Clutter in Chapter 2?

Acknowledge that you can overcome all obstacles and obtain all that you require. Why is it challenging for some people? Taking everything into account, mental chaos is the direct cause of this.

Mental confusion is thoughts, feelings, and tension gathered inside your head that cause you to become unstable, fight, stress, and divide yourself. A chaotic mind makes life difficult and perplexing. These things make us different from everyone else. Though invisible, mental confusion lurks where love and calm do not. We are against the regular flow and simplicity of life if we are disorganized. We're not allowing ourselves allowing ourselves to reach our full potential or realize the implications of who we are.

As I previously stated, you will demonstrate it in your life if you strongly believe your current position is correct. When your mind is disorganized, it becomes jumbled; many factors will push your mind in different directions. A voice may be telling you that it's all for naught. That's when you hear a different voice telling you you should never give up because it means everything to you. Finally, the question of which to pursue arises. Noting this will also be difficult.

In the unlikely event that you are not experiencing love, peace, and transparency, you are mentally ill. It exists only in your thoughts. Furthermore, all it takes is one unfavorable thought or emotion to lead you down a far more destructive path and be critical of yourself and others. There are currently eight accepted signs of mental disorder.

Chapter 3: Reasons for Mental Disarray

Several things can lead to mental congestion. It is important to assess psychological confusion before learning about these elements.

A man in the tale desired a painting hung on the wall. He didn't have a hammer, but he did have a nail. He then considered going to borrow a stick from his neighbor. Still, he began to mistrust himself.

Could it be that his neighbor wouldn't lend him his hammer? The day before, he hardly spoke to his neighbor. Maybe he was pressed for time. Perhaps he harbored resentment towards him. Given that he had done nothing wrong, why would he hold anything against him?

He would be happy to lend anything to his neighbor in need. Why, then, would he deny him access to a borrowed hammer? He reasoned that these kinds of people bring misery to others. Worse still, the hammer may make him feel he is dependent on him.

With these ideas in mind, the man raced over to his neighbor's house and insulted him before the neighbor knew why he had come to the door.

This narrative describes the mental congestion of an individual. The stuff that floats around in the mind of someone psychologically congested is called clutter. It is the reason he makes irrational and absurd leaps to conclusions.

Mental Disarray

Mental clutter refers to the junk that accumulates within your head. It could make you imagine the worst. It can leave you mired in a web of your creating and make you scared, worried, and pessimistic. It can also save you from a life of self-destruction, hardship, pain, estrangement, and anxiety. It may complicate and confuse your life. It may also cause you to become enmity with everyone.

Mental clutter is invisible to human sight. It also hides in regions devoid of peace and compassion. You will continue to oppose life's ease and flow the longer you are cluttered.

Your mind is clogged if you do not feel calm, love, and clarity. The clutter in your mind is exclusive and illusive. It starts as a vague and deceptive head. It develops into something larger and worse gradually but steadily.

The stories you tell yourself make up your mental clutter. These are the tales that undermine your well-being and hamper your potential. It tells you that you are unable, unfit, and unwilling. It makes you feel powerless by giving you cause for mistrust and doubt. Rather than telling you the truth about prosperity and abundance, it tells you lies about limitations and lack.

You turn into the man who needed a hammer and fell down the rabbit hole when it builds up, and you become blind to the reality of who you are, free of any restrictive beliefs. You start to feel that you are unworthy of love, not goodenough, and will never have what you desire. The truth comes out as you sort through this chaos.

3. Tidying up and decluttering equal minimalism

As we just saw, the leading proponents of minimalism as a way of life employ various strategies. Marie Kondo advocates tidying up before throwing away, whereas Fumio Sasaki takes the other tack and throws away before tidying. Given the connection between the two concepts, let's examine what is what.

Visualizing the equation is an intriguing approach to taking it all in:

Tidying up plus decluttering equals minimalism

Anyone looking for "minimalism" online, I assume, has realized they have a problem with accumulation in their lives. It can be an overabundance in their automobiles, homes, brains, computers, and smartphones. It should come as no surprise that there are many books on "decluttering" in all these areas.

The same is true for cleaning. Many people are trying to figure out how to arrange the tangible things they own. This explains why just as many books are available on organizing and cleaning one's home and life.

Recognizing the overlaps between these activities in any endeavor to live a minimalist lifestyle will be critical. Why could cleaning and organizing be the first steps toward a minimalist lifestyle? Let us examine these ideas and determine.

Decluttering is "the action of removing from a place those things you don't need in order to make that place more useful and pleasant," according to the Cambridge Dictionary. If that's the case, we have something that closely resembles the core principles of minimalism.

However, this concept refers to removal rather than precise discarding. Such comprehension seems difficult since "removing" just means taking anything away from a location; it doesn't indicate where things will end. It would be easy to relocate the many books strewn all over your living room and put them back on the appropriate shelves in your home library.

Therefore, there are two ways to look at the decluttering process: getting rid of things you don't want to keep and putting them back where they belong. From a minimalist perspective, decluttering entails parting with, discarding, and getting rid of items. This is what we discover in every available YouTube video and bestseller.

Where, then, is the distinction? Is a declutterer considered a minimalist? No, is the response. Although you may be drastically reducing the amount of stuff you maintain by decluttering, minimization necessitates a mental shift.

Decluttering can be done as a regular household clean-up or resolution for the new year. On the other hand, minimization is an ongoing process. Since they are not prone to collection, minimalists are extremely unlikely to have mountains of stuff that they need to regularly clear.

Organizing -

Organizing oneself seems like a logical next step after decluttering. The next step is thoroughly cleaning and arranging your space after removing everything cluttering it. There are numerous approaches to accomplish it. Since the MariKon phenomenon, the most widely used strategy is to focus on a single category at a time. Clothes, books, papers, and other items may fall under this category. Simply choose every item you own that falls into that category and arrange them together. Removing objects from shelves or drawers can allow you to see what has been in your space.

The amount of material we maintain without realizing it is astonishing. To help you decide what to keep and throw away, you must get everything out so you can see them. After that, a choice will be made regarding what belongs in the closets and drawers. And it will depend on how you feel about a specific item. Do you and that item still connect? Does that still have any use for you?

This is an extremely effective method of setting things aside that are no longer needed. Anything that remains in your home after you've cleaned it up is ready to be thrown out.

Your house is now successfully organized and decluttered. The same applies to other domains, such as your relationships, social media, car, and workspace. Everything neatly arranged will give you the much-needed breath of fresh air to begin living a minimalist lifestyle.

Cutting down

Once you've finished cleaning and decluttering, you'll have a lot of stuff that no longer has a place in your life. At that point, minimization becomes useful. The practical first step toward minimalism is removing the things you determine are superfluous. Remember that getting rid of these things physically is insufficient.

While sorting through your possessions, you also attempt to change your perspective from a condition of perpetual acquisition, exhibition, and accumulation to a new condition of necessity, purpose, and intentionality. Everything you throw away fits into the first category; the items you keep belong in the second.

Those who successfully maintain the necessities in all areas of their lives will be considered minimalists.

* * *

Some might choose to begin the procedure right away with a purge. That would depend totally on how each person handled it. I found it simpler to go in the order of minimization, decluttering, and tidying up because organizing my belongings allowed me to see what was missing from my room. The first indication that those things needed to go was that.

Even after I cleaned the place, those things remained unplaced. They needed to leave. I find this is a logical way to approach the process and a means of helping people emotionally detach from some things.

Making deliberate decisions about what to keep and discard is the foundation of minimalism. For me, the order I mentioned above was effective. I advise anyone searching for an efficient minimizing technique to do just that because it is simple to envision and implement.

Storage Areas: Garage, Basement, And Attic

The spaces where you will store whatever you decide to remove from your life will be the last areas you want to focus on during your minimalist journey. Why is this the last one? You likely underwent several months of minimalism before giving up on some of these items.

Get rid of it if you didn't miss it.

Some people find the attic challenging because it has everything from their Christmas decorations to dorm room supplies you haven't touched since college. Nowadays, most homes have a completed basement, which is typically quite tidy. You can ignore your husband's man cave if you consider going minimalist; he deserves his area.

Additionally, garages can be challenging. As previously mentioned, some people adopt a minimalism so extreme that they stop using their cars. Well done if you made it that far. If not, you should start by attempting to eliminate some of the unnecessary items in your garage.

Eliminating the Superfluous

We'll say it one more: get rid of anything you removed from your home and stored in the attic, cellar, or garage if you haven't missed it.

Take out the toys and office materials you don't use anymore, starting with your garage. Consider all the seasons and the things you utilize. Apply the same principles to your basement as you would to the rest of your house. If your basement serves only as storage, you should go through everything, box by box, once a year to see what you still need or use. The same holds for the attic. Save those decorations if you use them for Christmas every year. Throw it away if you used it for decoration five years ago but haven't used it since.

Still, there's a catch. Since you don't spend as much time in the attic or basement, it is preferable to store sentimental belongings there.

Easygoing

Going simple isn't possible if you're unwilling to part with some items. Working to free up as much floor space as you can before taking the cleaning game seriously is your best option. If you operate at a table or bench in your garage, make an effort to keep that space tidy. If you drive a car, you should also maintain a clean car area to avoid causing any harm.

Before entering and going through old shoes and pictures in a tote, you should concentrate on getting rid of larger stuff.

If you concentrate on your larger tasks, your work will seem easier to complete and like you are making progress. As you might have been collecting various items for decades, you should know that this area of your house will require the most time to complete. Going through ten years' worth of stuff isn't a fun rainy-day project.

Concentrate

Put most of your storage space into functional systems to improve your vision. Assign areas of the room to different seasons and memories. Keep everything as organized as possible using shelving or bins with obvious labels. Using this strategy, you can maintain as much room as possible while still having access to everything you need.

Hanging items in the garage is a great way to maximize the floor space available.

Simplifying this region of the house will probably cost you some money, but that's okay. You'll have a bit extra money to spend here because you'll save money elsewhere in the house.

Cut off

While the basement is a good spot for technology, the attic and garage are not the best places. But here's the twist: we advise bringing your technology with you now. We don't spend as much time in the basement, so feel free to have a working radio or television. Your body will naturally want to be in more open regions of the house, so you will use it less.

*Clutter five items each day.

Getting rid of stuff won't be a simple one-day task. The best strategy is to tackle it bit by bit. Every day, select five things (such as an extra pen, some socks, or something from your junk drawer) and put them in a designated spot. After a month, you can donate, sell for cash, or eliminate stuff you aren't using. Even if they are little steps, they form a habit that will eventually trigger significant change. Create a list of things to accomplish.

Making a to-do list is a great way to simplify and organize your life. No matter how chaotic your thoughts get, setting aside time to sit down and list your tasks can help you get through the storm. If you find it tough to focus on just one requirement due to many duties, writing it down in black and white will probably assist. Make a note of all the menial things you must do, like filing your taxes and cleaning your flat, in addition to your work and other commitments.

*Every day, dedicate 30 minutes to fitness.

Living healthy is just as important to minimalism as living with less. After all, staying well will benefit you if you value experiences over material belongings. Aim for at least 30 minutes of activity daily, but remember to adjust for your unique needs and fitness level. You will notice improvements in nearly every area of your life with just this one behavior. Put your attention where it's most needed, and give up worrying so much about what other people think of you. This issue affects a lot of people, some to the point of anxiety. You should maintain your composure and be happy with your identity, ideals, possessions, and actions. Strive towards this state, and don't let other people's judgments or expectations limit you. * Reducing your weight on other people's opinions will help you become more self-assured. Establish routines rather than making drastic changes.

Establishing routines is far more crucial than making drastic adjustments. You can drastically approach minimalism by packing all your extra items in the backyard, dousing them in petrol, and setting them all on fire. But doing so would prevent you from learning anything about how you relate to material possessions. It wouldn't be, either, and a year later, you would probably have another mound of junk. Instead, concentrate on forming the techniques above into habits, keeping in mind that this will need perseverance and continuous introspection.

Having Fun

Chapter 6: Knowing When to Give Up

People don't talk to each other very much these days, as anyone who has ever sat in a restaurant and watched people will attest. They act as though they are, but in reality, all they are doing is tapping feelings on their iPhones, completely unaware of the events they are taking on in the real world. Technology has captured our interest and taken over our lives to the point where we can no longer just be ourselves without it.

It's important to remember to spend more time outside and in nature while you're minimizing your life. Going back to nature and strolling through a forest or a flowing river has a particular quality that can help you solve your problems.

Nevertheless, people carry their computers, iPads, and cell phones with them, and they are constantly inundated with information. When it's appropriate, turn off your device. There are occasions when you should cut back on your interaction with the outside world, which includes using computers, iPads or tablets, radios, televisions, and cell phones:

when having dinner with others

When you pay a visit to your family

While having a talk

When visiting a park

When you're in a rural area

While at the seashore

The issue is that people can't turn off these gadgets and require some quiet time or, at the very least, organic discussion in their lives. During her visit to her mother in the hospital, a friend of mine would frequently slip outside to pass the time by checking her Facebook feed. She lost a great chance to say farewell to her mother, who passed away while she was having fun with her friends. We are too preoccupied with all the intrusions into our lives to be in fruitful partnerships.

Remorse is a major source of the emotional strain that people face nowadays. If a family member needs to talk, turning off the TV is far preferable. If you need to get something done, it's much better to turn off the phone. Having no Facebook account is preferable to prioritizing virtual pals over actual folks.

You find time to do things you would not have found time to do when you clear out all of this clutter from your life. You visit pals. Because you look past the smoke screen of what the outside world presents as entertainment, you communicate with others and become more productive as a member of your family and community.

Give yourself fixed hours if you work from home online so that you can still spend time with your family. Doing this makes you split your time more effectively and recognize that your time on the computer is work time. After working hours, you allow yourself to leave work behind and enjoy spending more time with your loved ones and friends.

Consider if you want to live in this kind of world the next time you witness a child ignoring you because he is too preoccupied with a video game. The next time you witness someone disregarding a companion because they are preoccupied with a tablet or phone conversation, consider whether you need everything. It's always going to be a no. Nobody's life should be so packed that genuine friendships and quality family time are impossible to find. Unless a voice on the other end of the queue is sufficiently essential, no one needs to give it precedence.

Declutteryour life by removing all the devices placed there to divert your attention from the true purpose of your existence. When you do, you discover that you are more in tune with life itself and that people will always be a part of your life regardless of these technologies, so you no longer need to call or message them on Facebook.

Consider what you believe to be true for yourself and hold onto that. The remainder is unnecessary. You have lost valuable time from all you spend watching the TV. Yes, retain the TV, but set watching limits and make the most of your time when it's on. Once you can release your life from the grip of technology, you can accomplish much more and not put off doing what you know you should. My life has changed since embracing a minimalist lifestyle, in my opinion. Because I have a greater purpose, I am more productive. I don't just happen to be successful; rather, I base my entire life around the minimalist philosophy, which makes achieving success easier.

Why So Many Individuals Are Only Able To Split Ways With Sorrow?

I've given you a general idea of what to expect if you adopt a minimalist lifestyle thus far. Your reading of the book thus far indicates your genuine interest in minimalism. You have to understand that everything has a drawback. For most people, separating from loved ones is already rather difficult.

Every lifestyle stems from an aspiration to reach a particular objective. The minimalist lifestyle aims to alter one's perspective on oneself and other things in addition to living as simply as possible. It is, after all, character training throughout. Most individuals find it difficult to live without consumer goods after a certain point. This could be due to various factors, some of which I will address below.

feelings

You own a lot of items with significant emotional worth. For instance, it brings to mind a certain circumstance or somebody. You have to determine for yourself what to preserve and what to sort out, as I have stated previously. It's not always essential to keep oneself apart from such things.

You can apply a small trick in this kind of circumstance. All of your sentimental belongings should go in a designated spot. After two to four weeks, see how often you have looked at and thought about these items. Using this method, you become aware of what matters to you and whether you need to remove items.

sentiments of guilt

Receiving anything as a Christmas or birthday gift is not unusual. Frequently from those who hold great significance in your life. You might feel bad about it even though you don't enjoy the object since you have a strong emotional attachment to that individual. You fear that giving this object away may cause you to trip and fall. When I tell you that you're not the only one who throws away gifts, it sounds difficult, but I think I can ease your guilt. Rarely would you accept a gift when it is offered to you. You accept it because the other person is delighted that you did. He wouldn't offer it to you if he didn't need it himself. The object does not need to be thrown in the trash immediately; it can be packaged and stored in a storeroom or similar location. You still have the option to return or give it away rather than throw it away. You won't face criticism from friends or family if you discard anything you received long ago. You can determine what to do with it because it's your house and your health. Is this person more interested in you being miserable with this object or happy without it? Who knows, maybe the present was even a poor purchase? Certainly not a suitable partner for cleaning the house with guilt.

Eventually.

Most of the time, it comes from frugal individuals who say they will eventually need a particular thing again. Most of this is just a pretext. Consider how often you've used that item over the past month if you find yourself using that justification.

Is he truly that significant?

Do you still need him?

It's advisable to schedule a time, and you can take care of the item if it's still not in use at home on that day.

The cost

Because a certain object is so costly, it is difficult to let go of it. Everyone has probably been in a similar circumstance at some point. But when you're cleaning out your flat, it's more important to consider each object's worth than its price. The price value and the personal value are unrelated. Like everyone else, you will possess something given to you for free or at very little cost but with great personal significance. For every object, therefore, ask yourself, "What is it worth to me?" and set aside the material criteria.

status symbol

You are also undoubtedly familiar with him—the ostentatious friend who feels compelled to show you his pricey possessions right away. One may argue that to live a minimalistic and mentally sound life; one must come to terms with the fact that material possessions can never truly add worth to oneself. Because no matter how many pricey things you have in your flat, this value will always be there. It is much simpler to detach from objects if you fully understand this base.

People struggle to separate themselves from objects for other reasons as well. Anything that you dump or discard automatically carries some danger. It is important to consider whether the risk is substantial and what the worst-case scenario would be. This lessens the anxiety associated with making errors. It's best to just let go and let the past behind you.

Clear Out Your Bedroom

Your bedroom ought to be the tidiest and most tranquil area out of all the rooms in your house. Since this is where you unwind at the end of the day, it should be peaceful and free of extra items.

Here, I'll assist you in organizing, cleaning, and creating the ideal sleeping environment. Since you are the only one who sees your bedroom, you may not be as concerned about keeping it clean as you should be. Most of the time, the bedroom easily turns into a dump for bags, clothes, washing, etc.

But that's not the right strategy and will hurt you personally. You should be able to unwind and fall asleep in your bedroom. Since there shouldn't be any debris or other obstructions preventing this, tidying up is necessary.

- Sorting the stuff in your bedroom into three heaps is necessary, just like in every other room you declutter. Sort items into three piles: one for items to be kept, one for stored somewhere else, and one for discard. The items you will retain should be few and limited to necessities or those that hold personal significance for you. We'll sort this pile into your room. Items that must be stored should be tucked away in the right spot in the house or packed into boxes. Before removing it, sorting the pile for donation, sale, or trash is necessary. You'll find the task easier if you label every package.

- Usually located inside the bedroom, your wardrobe or wardrobe needs to be thoroughly cleaned out. Since this is typically the messiest place in the room, it must be kept tidy. (This book offers a list of detailed wardrobe declutterings further on.) Keep only the clothes and accessories that you use; discard anything else. Keeping your wardrobe organized will make getting dressed in the mornings faster. Additionally, you ought to arrange your clothing by season. Store your non-seasonal clothing in a different closet so you may change it out when the appropriate time comes. There's no sense making a mess and hanging everything up. Make it a practice to reposition your clothing after undressing. Rehang the articles or properly place them in a laundry basket.

This includes any broken or unnecessary items in your room, such as furniture, artwork, or ornaments.

- Avoid storing extra furniture in the bedroom. A wardrobe, a bedside table, and your bed are generally plenty. Your bedroom will appear bigger and better the more floor space you can free up.

- Make sure everything is clean before organizing the things in your bedroom. Dust the furniture, shelf tops, and floors. The bedroom should be spotless from top to bottom. Clean out and empty each drawer and storage unit.

- The room's textiles, including the carpets, curtains, and bedding, should also be washed. At the very least, wash the bed linens and pillowcases once a week. Beds should be cleaned as often as possible because they tend to gather a lot of germs. While they don't require cleaning as frequently as bedding, curtains, and rugs, they still require careful maintenance. Every few months, try to get them dry-cleaned. This will guarantee that your bedroom is sanitary and spotless at all times.

- While you are performing the deep cleaning, check your mattress. Mattresses can accumulate a lot of bacteria or mold over time; if you cannot thoroughly clean them, get a new one. Your mattress should be vacuumed frequently and occasionally placed in the sun. Aim to keep mattresses for no more than seven or eight years. Make sure to give any white items in the room a thorough cleaning. More often than not, white objects will display dirt. For appropriate objects, use vinegar or bleach to help preserve their color.

Your room should be tidy and well-organized when you walk in. Avoid keeping a chair in which you overstock clothing. Put items away where they belong.

Refrain from hurling objects upon your bed as soon as you step inside. Your room will be more soothing for you if it is cleaner. Make use of tidy storage options to keep the area appearing neat.

Storage-configured beds are an excellent option. Any additional bedding and blankets for the season can be kept inside. These days, there are a lot of secret storage unit options accessible.

Purchase these to hide unwelcome items from view. Shelves are a fantastic tool for organizing your belongings. Such items can multiply over time, so try to keep them to a minimum in a bedroom.

To increase storage, purchase a bedside table with drawers. When you are done utilizing something, store it inside the drawers rather than piling it on the table. If you have kids, their rooms require much more storage than yours.

"I believe it is always best to be as minimalist as possible when it comes to accessories."

We will concentrate on your bedroom on the final day of the second week. Your sanctuary ought to be your bedroom. In your bedroom, you should always feel at ease, self-assured, and at ease. You should feel at ease and like you are in your safe place as soon as you walk into this area.

We suffer when our bedrooms are disorganized and untidy. Our stress levels rise, and we experience mental chaos as a result. Consequently, we frequently experience restless nights and consequent bodily discomfort. You may let go of all those stresses and bring calm back into your life by properly organizing and decluttering your bedroom.

Start by observing the obvious. All of the surfaces in the space should be cleaned, and whatever you have been storing on them should be sorted. Next, tidy up the floor. After that, empty each drawer. Lastly, tidy up the bed. Make sure to clear up your wardrobe if you have one. When cleaning an area, take everything out of it completely, arrange everything, and then put everything back in, just the really necessary things. All other items must be disposed of, donated, or arranged into a new home.

Keep your comfort and tranquility in mind while you reassemble your room.

Consider what furnishings and accents will add coziness and tranquility and discard everything else. Simplify your nightstands and dressers so that nothing can obstruct your access to the essentials. Make your bed, but avoid piling on too many pillows or other decorations. These are just pushed aside or end up on the floor so you can get to your bed at night. Simply replace what you need instead of holding onto the rest.

You can continue your daily responsibilities of tidying one surface, giving away one item, and journaling one entry once you have finished reorganizing your room. On the fourteenth day of your thirty-day challenge, you are then finished. Additionally, the second week of your challenge is now over. Take this opportunity to congratulate yourself on your accomplishments thus far!

Day 15

However, I cope with this by practicing meditation and realizing that my purpose in life is to help people. Living simply and avoiding excess is something I always have to remind myself to do in this materialistic world.

- Sandra Cisneros

You've probably discovered by now that there are a lot of items in your house that you've thought about getting rid of but are just unable to. How difficult it is to part with the things you love or previously adored could be dawning on you. We're going to concentrate on this feeling today. We will concentrate on establishing a rule that will enable you to process this feeling in a natural and efficient way.

You're going to learn how to sleep on it today. When you have anything that you're unsure whether to keep or part with, you will place it out in the open and leave it there till the following day. After giving it some thought, go to bed and execute your plan. It's not necessary to purge everything from your life. You will find solutions if you sleep on it or have trouble letting go of it. You will be able to determine for sure the following day if you are having difficulty letting go of anything or whether you are battling because you sincerely don't want to let go of it. After your response, you may decide whether to discard it or keep it in a secure location where it will stay valuable to you and remain organized.

Recall that the goal of minimalism is not to live with very little and to throw away everything you own. The goal is to make room for the things you need and want by eliminating the items you no longer need or want. It gives you the chance to enjoy life without being limited by material belongings and breaks free from the life of consumerism. However, that doesn't imply you can't own material goods. It's time to put the "sleep on it" strategy into effect if you have a crush on something but aren't sure if you should keep or part with it. Any of the things you have been having trouble with up to this point in your challenge can be used to accomplish this. You ought to try it with any other things in the future that give you trouble.

Take some time to finish your everyday tasks while working on implementing this new discipline. Put one thing in the donation bin, clean one surface, and complete your journal post for the day.

Changing One's Attitude And Discovering Balance

Living simply on a strict budget is not the goal of voluntary simplicity. To live in balance is to set higher standards. This is an intermediate path that avoids both extremes—poverty and excess. Actor in the media Duane Elgin

I'd believed for a long time that I needed to organize myself better. I just needed less stuff, I realize now. —Blogger and dietician AlysaBajenaru

Let's use three persons' experiences to examine minimalism's qualities and advantages. These three tales give the idea of minimalist human faces.

Conner's Story: From the Consumptive to the Conscious

Conner has a winning aura. He was raised in a middle-class home where hard effort was valued and expected of him to succeed. He must work for a global corporation, graduate with honors, and ascend to the top.

And he worked very hard! After working for a pharmaceutical company and graduating at the top of his class, he advanced to category manager in just four years. He is that talented.

As a result, Conner had little trouble repaying his education loans. He purchased an opulent home for his parents and himself and a high-end vehicle for his younger brother. He spends practically every evening dining out. He makes use of pricey club and gym subscriptions. He has been in a committed relationship with Mina, his college sweetheart, with whom he presents jewelry to her nearly every month. His graduate school and workplace friends look up to him greatly.

However, he senses something is wrong deep inside. Occasionally, he wakes up feeling anxious rather than at ease as he strolls around his flat holding a mug of freshly brewed coffee. He occasionally gets overburdened by his daily commitments and appointments while driving. He seems to be living the life of a reality program called Keeping Up with Conner.

His credit card debt is still accruing, in addition to his mortgage and auto loan payments, which is not helping. Every year, his pay rises dramatically, and he receives quarterly incentives that are determined by his performance and the performance of his team and the business. He makes twenty times as much money overall as his college pals do. But it's insufficient in some way. His salary rises in tandem with his purchases and way of living. He feels a stirring inside him to make a change in his life. However, he was too concerned and busy to listen to that inner voice.

Mina recommended they take a trip after noticing he had been under too much stress lately. He immediately accepted and made reservations for a week-long vacation at an upscale resort on a Caribbean island. It was a wonderful and relaxed vacation with a few exceptions—dinners and evenings when Conner had to attend to pressing business. He would not stop looking at his phone while they were out on a boat in the water. It appears that he was mind-hopping in addition to island-hopping.

Things had returned to normal when they got home. Conner continued to feel energized. That's when Mina first exposed him to Joshua and Ryan and their 21-day minimalist challenge and lifestyle.

Conner completed a three-month restoration program and reassessed his lifestyle with assistance from Ryan, Joshua, and Mina. He made little daily adjustments to his lifestyle and mentality until minimalism became second nature to him, and he lived it rather than consumed it.

He cleaned his home. After two weeks, he sold or gave away clothing, appliances, equipment, furniture, and other items he had not used. He got rid of things that weren't working. After three months, he eventually sold his large home and moved into one of the main rooms of the home he had bought for his parents.

He decluttered his automobile and threw away receipts, empty bottles, and other junk gathered over the years. He also discovered currency and coins inside his trunk. He eventually sold his vehicle. Instead, he purchased a simple motorbike. He's always wanted to ride a bike across cities!

Because he enjoyed his profession, he continued to work in an office. However, he dropped the specifics. He began to assign his teammates extra tasks. He realized that he had been doing tasks that his coworkers could complete. He found that juniors can perform some managerial functions. They even go above and beyond his expectations at times. He was an excellent mentor and time manager.

Along with reviewing his finances, he created a budget. He set aside percentages for contributions, future and retirement planning, savings, investments, everyday expenses, leisure, and debt settlement. He also made a good living by selling things he didn't need and gave the money he made from that sale to his alma mater's scholarship fund.

He now gave his health more attention. He no longer visits the gym nearly daily and concentrates on his overall wellness. It involves not only physical activity but also proper diet and rest. As a result, he cooks healthier meals at home more often, sleeps for six hours every night rather than for just two, and works out for fifteen minutes every day rather than spending two hours every day at the gym.

In addition, he spends many hours on the weekends preparing and cooking meals for the week with his parents and fiancée. He found that he enjoys cooking and is quite skilled in the kitchen. He once delighted his coworkers by bringing in a pan of delectable dark chocolate brownies and a container of rich beef stew for everyone.

That he was the one who prepared and baked the treats startled them. As he chewed the brownies, his supervisor yelled, "Conner, is there something that you can't do?" He laughed and said, "Yeah, I can't stop being so good at this." The brownies and beef stew made them giggle a lot.

Three months later, he is more content and energized. He no longer gets his confidence from external possessions but rather from within.

Conner came to several realizations during this change. He realized he had more than enough and didn't need it anymore. He came to realize that his relationships are the most important thing. He now sees his folks more frequently. He prepares and joins them for dinner.

He was also taken aback by Mina's unwavering support in the face of his mood swings, and he will always be grateful to her for introducing him to this basic way of living. He will never be the same because of how she altered his life. He likes her and the great energy she carries with her everywhere she goes because she positively impacts his life. After he recently proposed to her, they are getting ready for their wedding next year. Rather than having a large wedding, they prefer to keep it small and intimate.

Stan, his brother and the man who will be best man at the wedding became intrigued by this minimalist trend as well. Conner is working closely with him over this first week as he embarks on his personal adventure. Their shared link has become one of simplicity.

Conner's story is touching and inspirational, don't you think?

Chapter 2: Establish Your Budget for Minimalism

It's time to create your minimalist budget now that you have evaluated your financial condition.

Determine your essential spending by considering your priorities, values, and objectives. Pay attention to the expenses associated with necessities such as housing, utilities, food, transportation, and debt repayment. Spend as little as possible on luxuries that don't fit your priorities.

Next, create a budget structure for your particular expenses by dividing your spending into typical categories. Categories give resources a structure so that needs can be met before wants. Amounts should be allocated to necessary costs such as housing and debt repayment. Then, as you see fit, allocate the remaining monies among the variable expenses.

Set boundaries for more malleable categories, such as shopping, entertainment, and eating. Here, limit overspending by establishing a monthly cap that necessitates careful planning by automating regular and necessary costs to be paid on schedule.

Employ the 50/30/20 budgeting strategy: allocate 50% to necessities, 30% to luxuries, and 20% to debt repayment and savings. Adapt percentages to your unique circumstances and priorities. For example, temporarily switch to a 60/20/20 split if you have a lot of debt.

Don't plan for every last cent. Monthly wriggle room should be allowed in several categories. When necessary, savings from one area might be used to make up for overages in another. The aim is not perfection but congruence with priorities.

Prioritise saving for monthly goals before spending on desires. Over time, even tiny automatic contributions add up to significant outcomes. Start by saving more for emergencies, then increase your retirement, college, and other savings.

Lastly, welcome financial adaptability. Review monthly spending and make any necessary adjustments to category levels to keep on track. It's acceptable if your budget from today isn't flawless. Adjust when your financial circumstances change over time. Focused on the essentials, minimalist budgeting is easy to use and straightforward. Now that you have your customized budget plan, it's time to start paying attention to how much you spend. Let's get started on cost optimization and developing reliable financial practices.

Prioritise Needs Over Wants By Focusing On Essential Expenses.

Any minimalist budget's cornerstone separates needs from wants and prioritizes the most important costs. Needs include fixed expenses for subsistence and fundamental wellbeing, such as housing, utilities, food, insurance, and the minimal amount of debt serviced each month. Wants are extra costs for convenience, leisure, and lifestyle choices.

Prioritize allocating funds to your demands and financial commitments while developing your budget. Prioritize paying for necessities over wants. This guarantees that you can pay for necessities like food and shelter no matter how much additional money you have each month.

residing

The largest expense on your budget should be your rent or mortgage payment. One essential need is a stable place to live. Have I paid for housing in full for the month before I allocate funds to any other category? Add up all related housing expenses, such as utilities like gas and electricity, property taxes, renters insurance, and maintenance expenditures. Spending more on a place that suits your family's needs is acceptable. Just make sure it fits into your budget.

Moving

Most individuals depend on reliable transportation to work, do errands, and handle daily duties. Prioritize paying your insurance and auto payments each month. Set aside money for supplies, maintenance, gas, and registration. Plan for bus or metro passes if you use public transportation frequently.

Food

A basic physiological need is food. Set up enough money for wholesome groceries to feed your family for the duration. Planning your meals helps reduce eating out. Set aside some cash for occasional takeout and snacks. Just don't skimp on those necessary supermarket basics.

Protection

Having life, health, disability, and other essential insurance guarantees, you are financially secure against life's unforeseen events. Make these monthly payments non-negotiable.

Paying Off Debt

Always make the bare minimum payment on your debts, even if it means making a sacrifice. Pay down any past-due balances immediately and make aggressive principal reductions. Invest as much as you can on high-interest debt.

Conserve

After you've taken care of your immediate requirements, start saving money for things like retirement, college, and health care. Little automated savings installments made each month build up rapidly. Everything else in your budget, such as entertainment, eating out, and indulgent shopping, belongs in the wants section. Don't spend money on things until you've paid for your necessities and savings. Following this rule will guarantee that you can succeed regardless of your money.

Assess Desires

When creating a wants budget, use greater leeway. These costs frequently provide short-term benefits but little lasting worth. If money is tight, spend less on Expensive cable packages, frequent dining out, upscale cosmetic procedures, opulent trips, and season tickets.

Club memberships, Boat/RV costs.

Do not deprive yourself. However, carefully weigh each desire against conflicting priorities. Is spending $50 on this product a better fit for my values than putting that money toward paying off debt or investing for retirement?

Sort your wants according to priority. Pay modestly for top-tier desires. When necessary, temporarily give up lower-level desires to meet financial objectives sooner. The fundamental idea of minimalist money management is to separate needs from wants and to budget appropriately.

15. Being Correct All the Time

It's common advice to always do the right thing. But that's just not feasible at all. A strong argument typically supports every significant choice someone makes. For example, when someone lies to you about the state of your dying father, it's not because he wants to keep something from you. He may be trying to keep you from being depressed.

Solution:

Delay passing judgment on people's behavior.

Remain receptive to their justifications for their actions.

Admit your wrongdoings honestly as well.

16. Fantasy of Fairy Tales

Many individuals are raised on tales of heroes and heroines who ultimately come out on top. Although it's good that they instill optimism in you, they might also brainwash you to believe in fairy tales. This type of cognitive distortion is the wish that everything would work out for your ultimate success. This includes your strong conviction that something or someone will come to your aid in time.

Solution: Believe in yourself, work hard, and accept the results of your efforts, good or bad. You don't always win; sometimes you do. Seek aid rather than waiting for it to appear out of nowhere.

Acknowledging your mistakes in thought goes beyond only preventing and reducing mental clutter. It can also help you avoid acquiring tangible clutter. It's not necessary to hoard beauty items just because you think you're ugly. Ads may not always indicate that you should purchase a product. You don't have to get every official memorabilia just because you think something is great.

Overcoming Self-Doubt

Self-doubt is being unsure of your abilities, intentions, decisions, and behaviors. It's easiest to define as the voice in your brain that poses queries like, "Can you do it?" Are you competent enough? Did you complete it correctly? The voice in your head is a type of mental clutter that prevents you from taking action and realizing your goals. It can imply that you are now too attached to your material belongings to truly implement minimalism in your life.

It's not all bad to be doubtful. Typically, it serves as a source of constraint. It prevents employers from appointing unfit candidates. It keeps a professional in advertising from launching campaigns hurriedly. Self-doubt operates similarly. Self-doubt may be both a potential ally and an enemy since it forces you to be conscious of your limitations.

Self-doubt can be an ally when used for self-improvement and self-preservation under difficult circumstances. You feel dissatisfied with your life as a result.

Being aware of your advantages and disadvantages might help you get over self-doubt and lead the life you choose. Although you are capable of doing anything, you can still take action. You can always improve yourself if you're not good at something.

You can reflect on the moments in the past when you felt bad about questioning yourself. You could be inspired to trust yourself this time by those regrets. You can also reflect on the instances when you tried despite your doubts. Despite what your inner voice tells you, unless it's immoral or against the law, people don't care what you do or say.

Try viewing your previous failures differently if you have experienced them. Even though you were unsuccessful, you might have gained knowledge. If nothing else, you're not lamenting not giving it a shot.

You should also consider how your current circumstance differs from your previous one. Even though you were inexperienced formerly, you've improved greatly since then.

Putting Values First

Resolving self-doubt can also be achieved by concentrating on your priorities. Is it worth missing out on a fantastic chance because you're afraid you won't succeed?

Journaling and meditation are beneficial. Decide what matters most to you via meditation. Don't complicate your meditation. It's unnecessary to purchase audiobooks, download white noise, or buy expensive mats. You can choose a calm area of your home, settle in, and allow your thoughts to appreciate the simplicity of your surroundings. Consider the thoughts bugging you a few minutes or hours ago after that. Combat every pessimistic notion. Concentrate on something constructive, ideally your principles. Re-enter the present moment by paying attention to your environment.

Next, list your precise objectives that align with your values. Put them in writing in your journal. Update your progress once a week. Remind yourself of your progress whenever doubts and other pessimistic ideas enter your head. You can choose a new objective once the previous one has been reached.

The Religion of Ease and Convenience

Naturally, one of our most artificial desires is ease and comfort. Our goal is for everything to proceed as swiftly and smoothly as possible. It should come as no surprise that we would pay more for comfort and convenience when we could save a tonne of money for something that would be somewhat less convenient but slightly more uncomfortable.

Americans spend their hard-earned money on pre-cut fruit and vegetables because they don't want to deal with washing, slicing, and dicing their produce, much alone finding a knife and chopping board. Their time is far too valuable. They would thus spend a good deal of money on pre-cut components.

This has turned into a sophisticated economic cult. People seem to think they have a right to this, and in addition to being prepared to spend more, any assault on ease and comfort is viewed as abnormal, peculiar, odd, and even inhuman.

To fill this personal emptiness and maintain economic growth, consumers must feel alienated from the system for them to continue making purchases.

The final straw is that each of the fictions above leads to the same outcome. Individuals feel alienated if they believe these fictions, which is true for most individuals.

You'll be continuously running on that treadmill if you think your needs will change the following year and that you should change how you buy things. You'll just need to buy one set of things after another or chase after one trend after another.

Individuals have a sense of alienation, and what's interesting is that they have no idea why, having fallen for the lies presented above. From the standpoint of the contemporary economy, though, clients must feel excluded. They must believe that they would be incomplete without other items. They needed more possessions or prestige to be happy and grow in confidence.

Naturally, the goal is to alienate as many people as possible so that they will be able to continue consuming. The economy continues to thrive as a result. Every year, it simply keeps pushing it to the next frontier.

The question is, when will it end? When will people understand that most of this is unnecessary fluff? Worst of all, in their pursuit of comfort and ease, they feel smaller and smaller, less and less in control, and more helpless.

You have to get over these.

You are reading this book with a different goal in mind. You are weary of the never-ending consumer cycle. You want to overcome the fictions mentioned above to have a brighter future for yourself.

There are two things you must comprehend. First of all, you are not your belongings, your vehicle, the clothes you wear, or the perfume you wear. You are a unique individual.

Despite the common belief that residents of a certain address possess certain qualities, you are not your address. Do you recall Beverly Hills 90210? People have certain expectations when you tell them you live on Park Avenue in New York.

You are not your status, secondly. This isn't who you are, regardless of what other people may think of you, because you hang out with the right people, purchase the right things, or travel in the appropriate circles. Despite the opinions of many, you are an individual with a distinct personality or identity.

Remember that declaring one's independence from the approval of others equates to being able to break free from status. People are erratic, so think again if you believe you can't survive without their approval. Even if they adore you now, you might be a pile of garbage to them in the future. That's just the nature of human beings.

Is it really what you want to rely on? Is it truly worth putting your own mental health and wellbeing at risk for the approval of others? Do you want to be at the mercy of individuals you cannot control?

Control is lost when one's identity is based on flawed mental habits and programming.

So why are suicide rates in the industrialized world so high? These are individuals from median households with annual incomes between $80,000 and $100,000. These individuals and those from households with far higher incomes ought to be the happiest members of society if the logic of the contemporary economy and its social structures is right.

It turned out to be the opposite. It turns out that in some situations, having more money puts you at greater risk. People who commit themselves while wealthy and well-off are not hard to find. Despite being admired and worshipped by many, there is no shortage of those who despise who they are and feel so alone and rejected. Many individuals are envious of them or wish they could be like them.

What is happening, then? The crux of the issue lies in the absence of control if you base your contentment on events and circumstances beyond your control. There are a lot of uncontrollable situations in this world, and the difficulty lies in the fact that once you become addicted to the rush, it might be difficult to break the habit.

If the source of your happiness and self-worth is outside of your control, this will become a problem. You can't control your external surroundings, so you want to keep hitting that button to keep these positive feelings coming. However, you can't do that. Its thoughts and agenda are its own.

What takes place with you? You become reliant on outside circumstances, which are regrettably beyond your control. You've been trained to stay on the treadmill to keep the system running. You're the one who continuously feeds money into the system to keep it going for millions and millions of other people. The depressing truth is that happiness gets harder and harder to maintain.

A person who dies contentedly, having taken the time to smell the roses, is likely to have many more happy memories than someone who is just in a constant rush to experience and acquire everything. Ultimately, it's essentially simply a wish list. What now? Savor the journey and witness life in all its splendor and horror. That is life itself. It's a combination. Accept it or go forward.

Begin with yourself.

In what ways can you simplify your life? This could be the simplest or the hardest step, depending on you. If you believe this will be the hardest step for you, you might want to go to the next part and return to this later. On the other hand, starting with oneself can help you become more self-aware, making your future work easier as you work toward a simpler, happier life.

Approaching the inside from the outside, start there. In what ways can you "minimize" your life? Do you brush your hair for ten minutes every day? It can grow out and be worn in a ponytail, or you could want to chop it short. Do you struggle to decide what to wear every day for a while? Choosing to dress simply and prioritize your comfort over the newest trends is something you might want to consider doing consciously. Do you shave for twenty minutes every day or just once a week? It could be your desire to grow a beard and eliminate the inconvenience of shaving.

On the other hand, if you have a long, bushy beard that gathers everything from cookie crumbs to glitter, and you're sick of having to comb it out and apply oil, you might want to consider purchasing a basic electric razor to simplify your daily care. Do you accessorize with jewelry? Even while it might only take 30 seconds to put on and remove your favorite necklace in the morning and evening, if you wear it every day, you'll be wasting six hours a year adjusting it. Would it make more sense for you to always wear the necklace? Beard oil and necklaces might seem insignificant, but little things add up. Five or six insignificant daily tasks can soon add too much time. In the long run, you will save more time, money, and energy if you can be more aware of these small details that you can change with small adjustments. Start with your appearance, as you will be able to see your progress staring back at you every day in the mirror if your appearance is in line with your goals.

What about your trinkets? Do you carry a large purse stuffed with rarely used items and have no idea what is hidden inside? Take everything out of your purse, including unnecessary items. Choose a smaller purse so you won't be able to fill it with unnecessary items you'll have to carry about all day. Go through your wallet and get rid of everything unnecessary if you want it to explode, as George Constanza did on Seinfeld when he accidentally put one more piece of paper inside (FREE FIRST LESSON: LEARN GUITAR!). Get rid of those bits of paper if you secretly know you'll never take that guitar lesson or claim that Save the Pandas poster! My wallet collected those little bits of paper over the better part of fourteen years. When I emptied my last wallet, do you know how many of those bits of paper I required or even recognized? No more than one or two. Clear out the small bits of paper in your bag, wallet, pocketbook, and other items. Why add more weight to what you already have to carry daily?

Proceed to the interior now, to your mind. Your ideas. For you, as it is for me, this might be the hardest part. Finding the thoughts that aren't helping you is the first step toward streamlining your thinking. "I can't" or "I won't" are common precursors to thoughts that impede your progress and cause unnecessary stress. For example, "I can't get rid of my DVDs!" I can't continue to live that way! This lifestyle doesn't seem like it's for me! We are frequently the worst adversaries of our limiting notions. You won't likely ever attempt if you don't believe it's feasible or even viable for you. Even though I know these ideas, they still cross my mind. I thought I had gotten rid of most of the "I don't," "it won't," and "I can't" thoughts, but my friend called attention to the fact that I was still thinking them and expressing them in my speech throughout our conversation, and I wasn't even aware of it. Adverse thoughts are like tiny anchors that do nothing but drag you down and prevent you from moving forward. Get rid of them! Change them out for thoughts and phrases that are empowering. Always be on the lookout! The more aware of this issue you are, the more equipped you'll be to respond with "why can't I?"

You might always battle with this, just as I sometimes do when facing fresh ideas and thoughts. But consider this: How can I accomplish this instead of thinking, "I can't"?And at least you won't have given up trying, regardless of whether you can solve the problem. Always try something and give it a shot rather than giving up completely. Our most valuable lessons come from our mistakes. At that point, will you give up or apply the lessons you gained from your defeat to enter the ring again for round two?

Reduce the complexity of your ideas and eliminate those that will simply hinder you or serve no use. This can be challenging. Years may pass, but everything is achievable if you have the correct mindset—one that welcomes opportunities rather than closes them. Now, tell yourself you will learn a lot and save money and time on your road toward minimalism. Then, put your words into action and start living your dream.

Have You Set A Time Restriction For The Meeting?

15 to 60 minutes is the recommended duration. Set a timer and ensure you don't start more work than you can finish in the allotted time. Stop when the timer goes off, tidy up, and then take a short break—say, fifteen minutes. It's imperative to take a break to avoid burnout. After your break, you might always choose to give it another shot or not.

One room at a time, concentrate.

Feeling overwhelmed when cleaning your home is quite simple since you may believe the entire space needs to be decluttered. You could easily become discouraged and begin decluttering due to this feeling. Declutter one room at a time and, if at all possible, divide the space into smaller portions to prevent this. For example, you can divide the bedroom into areas like the closet, dresser, nightstand, bed, etc., if you wish to declutter it. When you declutter the kitchen, you can set up areas for the pantry, cabinets, refrigerator, kitchen counter, drawers, and other items. In this manner, you won't feel pressured to finish everything at once and be more inclined to persevere until the entire house is decluttered.

As you go through each chamber, make three piles on the ground. These will fit into the boxes with labels. After picking up each object, decide which box it belongs in and quickly put it inside it.

Here are some illustrations of decluttering:

Clear out your closet: Based on statistical data, we wear about 20% of our wardrobe 80% of the time. This implies that most of us have overstuffed closets full of items we either don't wear or don't fit well anymore.

Get rid of any toys your kids aren't using. Too frequently, we err on the side of "more is better," especially regarding our children. Most Americans buy far more toys than their children would ever need, meaning our children don't need to be creative or develop their improvisational skills. Remove most of the toys and save the ones your children play with. But before you do this, it will be wise to speak with your kids.

Delete the copies: Don't forget to discard duplicates when tidying each room. Place the second measuring cup in a box if you have any.

Make room for everything: Find a home for anything you intend to keep. Because there isn't a single location where everything can be kept, ensuring each item has a specific area to be maintained helps prevent things from ending up everywhere. Since everyone knows to put things back where they belong after usage, this will also stop clutter from building up.

Vacuum and clean the room: Nothing makes a place feel fresher than a thorough cleaning. Examine the neat space, which you might not have had the opportunity to see in months or perhaps years.

How to Turn Everything into Minimalism

Being a minimalist takes careful planning. This is the process of organizing and decluttering your life. Above all, it is an ongoing practice or habit. It is impossible to clear all the clutter in one sitting and then forget about it. After a few days, similar junk will start to appear. You must adhere to a procedure to recognize clutter and prevent it from reentering your life.

Establish Rules

One size does not fit all when it comes to becoming a minimalist. You'll need to establish guidelines that suit your needs. It will be necessary for you to identify the items that are cluttering your life the most and to take a systematic approach to getting rid of them.

There are different rules for decluttering your house, office, and personal life. Every sector requires distinct care. As a result, after you have reduced the amount of possessions, you will need to determine how you want your life to appear.

Keep Your Concentration

Over time, we develop the habit of collecting stuff. Letting go of wanting to hold onto things is not easy. Everything in our lives has a purpose. It is common to feel they would come in handy later on while cleaning. All of the clutter is a result of this temptation. It will be necessary for you to resist the urge and continue cleaning.

Arrange

Having easy access to crucial items is the main goal of minimalism. Even if you have a few items, you might not be able to get them if you are not organized properly. It's critical to assign significant items in your house a correct location. Keeping those items in the same location must become second nature to you. Retrieval is made simple by this.

Utilizing everything you own to its greatest potential is the practice of minimalism. It could appear tough at first to part with items. When you need them, it will be a huge relief to discover the essentials there. This is only possible if you begin to give them the respect they deserve, which will be difficult if you have many of them.

www.ingramcontent.com/pod-product-compliance
Lightning Source LLC
Chambersburg PA
CBHW052142110526
44591CB00012B/1821